I0518729

When Life Feels Heavy

Finding Light, Comfort and Hope One Gentle Step at a Time

Patricia Hylton

DBIH ENTERPRISES, LLC

Copyright © 2026 Patricia Hylton

All rights reserved.

No part of this publication may be reproduced, stored, or transmitted in any form or by any means — electronic, mechanical, photocopying, recording, or otherwise — without prior written permission from the author, except for brief quotations used in reviews or scholarly works.

For permissions or inquiries, contact:

info@DBIHEnterprises.com

All Scripture quotations (if used) are from publicly available translations and remain the intellectual property of their respective publishers.

Cover design direction by Patricia Hylton.

Interior content created and developed in collaboration with AI writing assistance.

Printed in the United States of America.

ISBN: 979-8-9942787-0-3

Published by:

DBIH Enterprises, LLC

www.DBIHEnterprises.com

Disclaimer

T his book is a resource for emotional support and personal reflection.

It is not intended to replace professional mental health care, medical treatment, therapy, counseling, or crisis intervention.

If you are experiencing severe emotional distress, thoughts of self-harm, or a mental health emergency, please contact:

988 Suicide & Crisis Lifeline (U.S.)

Crisis Text Line: Text HOME to 741741 (U.S.)

Your local emergency number outside the U.S.

The author and publisher assume no responsibility for the misuse or misunderstanding of the information contained in this book.

This book is offered with compassion and care — but it is not a substitute for professional help.

Dedication

To the ones who are hurting, who are grieving, who are lonely, and who are trying their best to make it through each day—this is for you. May these pages be a soft place to land and a quiet reminder that you are not alone.

Preface

From the Author:

There are seasons in life that feel heavier than words can hold.

Seasons where the holidays bring more ache than joy, where memories feel sharper than celebration, and where your heart whispers questions you don't know how to answer.

I wrote this book for those seasons.

Not because I have all the answers — I don't.

But because I've walked through my own dark nights, my own confusing transitions, my own waves of grief and loneliness, and I know what it feels like to wish for something steady to hold on to.

This book is that steady place.

It's not meant to rush your healing.

It's not meant to fix what happened.

It's not meant to tell you to "be strong" or "think positive."

It's meant to sit with you.

To steady you.

To remind you that your feelings make sense — and that pain does not get to write the final chapter of your story.

As you read...breathe.

Pause when you need to.

Take your time.

Come back to the chapters that feel like home.

Let the words wrap around you with warmth and gentleness.

You're not walking this season alone.

— Pat

How To Use This Book

This book is meant to be a companion — not a sprint, not a challenge, not a checklist.

Use it slowly.

Use it honestly.

Use it in the way your heart needs it in this season.

Here's how:

1. You don't need to read it in order. Skip around. Return to the chapters that speak to you. Use the table of contents to find what fits the moment you're in.

2. Read in small sections. The chapters are intentionally short and comforting. Even reading one page can be grounding.

3. Pause when your emotions rise. Don't push through. Give yourself permission to step away and breathe.

4. Use the Reflection Prompts. These questions help your heart catch up with your mind.

5. Pair the book with the emotional tools. Your Emergency Kit, grounding practices, and micro-movements can be used anytime — not just when reading.

6. Come back as often as you need. This book is designed to be reread during hard moments. Let it be a familiar voice in seasons of overwhelm.

7. Let the process be gentle. Healing takes time. Move at your pace.

Contents

Introduction

For the One Who Feels Heavy This Season

The holidays have a way of magnifying everything — the joy, the laughter, the traditions, the lights. But they also magnify the ache. The emptiness. The memories. The shadows of what used to be, or what you wish could be.

Maybe this year feels heavier than you expected.

Maybe you've lost someone you never imagined spending a holiday without.

Maybe life has let you down in ways you're still trying to understand.

Maybe your heart is carrying disappointments that no one else can see.

Or maybe — and this one is tender — you've just felt lonely in a way that's hard to put into words.

If that's you, hear me clearly:

There is nothing wrong with you.

You're not broken.

You're not weak.

You're not "failing the holidays."

You're simply human. And being human means some seasons feel heavier than others.

This book isn't here to force you into joy.

It's not here to tell you to "cheer up" or "choose happiness."

And it's definitely not here to make light of what you're carrying.

It's here to sit beside you — gently, honestly — with a soft blanket of comfort and clarity.

It's here to whisper back hope in the exact places your heart feels thin.

Because even when your world feels dim...

there is a light that hasn't gone out.

It may be quiet.

It may be small.

But it's there — in you, around you, and waiting to guide you forward.

Some people call that light hope.

Some call it steady resilience.

Some call it the presence of God — that quiet peace that shows up not in fireworks, but in a hush.

This book doesn't require you to be deeply spiritual to feel something shift inside you.

But it does want you to know:

You're not walking through this season alone. Not for one moment.

This is a gentle journey — a hand on your shoulder, a warm cup in your hands, a nod that says,

"I see you. And you're allowed to take this one day at a time."

So breathe.

Settle in.

Let's walk through this together — slowly, compassionately, honestly.

Not to rush your healing, but to help you rediscover the light that's been quietly waiting inside you all along.

"You're not failing the holidays.
The holidays just look different
when your heart is healing."

Chapter 1:

When the Holidays Feel Heavy

The world loves to paint the holidays as magical — snow that sparkles, families that get along, tables full of food, laughter echoing through cozy rooms, twinkling lights, warm cocoa. And for some people, that's real.

But for others — maybe for you — the holidays bring a different kind of energy.

A heaviness.

A quiet ache.

An emotional pressure you didn't ask for.

It's like the whole world is singing while you're trying to keep your heart from breaking open.

You're surrounded by decorations and cheerful commercials... but inside, something feels off.

Empty.

Tender.

Raw.

And here's the truth most people never say out loud:

The holidays don't create loneliness or grief — they just reveal it.

They bring it to the surface.

They hold up a mirror to whatever your heart has been quietly carrying all along.

They shine a spotlight on the empty chair at the table, the tradition that isn't the same, the relationship that shifted, or the version of yourself you miss.

You're not imagining it.

You're not being "dramatic."

You're not oversensitive.

You're responding to real losses, real disappointments, real changes.

> *"The holidays amplify what the*
> *heart whispers all year long."*

Why This Time of Year Feels So Intense

Let's slow this down, because understanding your emotional landscape doesn't take your pain away — but it does help you breathe inside it.

There are four big reasons the holidays hit harder:

1. Expectations Are Louder Than Reality

Movies, music, social media, family traditions — they all preach one message:

"This is the season to be joyful."

But what happens when your season isn't joyful?

When you're grieving?

When money is tight?

When relationships are strained?

When you miss someone?

When you feel disconnected?

The gap between expectation and reality can feel like a wound.

2. Old Memories Wake Up

Smells.

Songs.

Places.

Decorations.

They're emotional time machines.

You hear a song from childhood and suddenly grief hits you in the chest.

You unpack an ornament and your eyes fill with tears.

You sit in a room full of people but feel strangely alone.

This isn't weakness.

It's memory.

It's love trying to find a place to land.

3. Loneliness Gets Louder at Night

During the holidays, evenings can feel longer.

Quieter.

Emptier.

Your brain interprets that stillness as loneliness, even if you've been around people all day.

This is a normal biological response — you're not "too emotional." You're wired for connection.

4. You're Carrying Emotional Weight No One Can See

Grief.

Disappointment.

Disconnection.

Lost dreams.

Identity shifts.

Breakups.

Estranged relationships.

Burnout.

Exhaustion.

You've been strong for so long...

and this season just pulls back the curtain.

What You're Feeling Is Valid

Let me say this plainly:

If the holidays feel heavy, it doesn't mean you're ungrateful.

It means you're human.

And humans feel.

We remember.

We grieve.

We long.

We hope.

We ache.

We heal.

You are not the odd one out.

You're not "ruining the season."

And you don't have to pretend your heart is somewhere it isn't.

This chapter — and this book — gives you permission to honor what's true without apology.

Because healing begins with honesty.

> *"You're allowed to feel what you feel without performing joy for anyone."*

You're Not Alone — Even When You Feel Like You Are

Loneliness during the holidays doesn't always look like sitting in an empty house.

Sometimes it looks like sitting in a room full of people and feeling invisible.

Sometimes it looks like being the one who "keeps everyone else together" while quietly falling apart inside.

Sometimes it looks like scrolling through photos of others laughing — while you wonder why no one notices your silence.

Loneliness is not about proximity.

It's about connection.

And during the holidays, connection can feel complicated.

Maybe the people you used to lean on aren't close anymore.

Maybe you're surrounded by family, but no one really gets you.

Maybe you've outgrown certain relationships.

Maybe you're grieving the one person who always made you feel seen.

Or maybe... this year changed you in ways you're still trying to explain.

If any of that feels familiar, breathe this in:

Your loneliness does not mean you are unlovable.

It does not mean no one cares.

It does not mean you are forgotten.

It means you're carrying a tender part of your heart into a season that demands smiles and sparkle.

It means you're human in a season that sometimes forgets the human heart has limits.

And even if you feel alone, you are not alone in the experience of loneliness.

More people carry this ache than you can imagine — but like you, they hide it beneath sweaters, schedules, and "I'm fine."

Holiday loneliness is a quiet epidemic — and this book is your safe space to finally admit the truth:

"This is hard.

And it's okay that it's hard."

> *"Loneliness is not a reflection of your worth. It's a reflection of your need for connection — a need every human shares."*

The Truth About Grief During the Holiday Season

Grief doesn't follow a calendar.

It doesn't wait for January.

It doesn't pause because the world strings up lights and expects celebration.

If anything, grief gets louder.

Because the holidays bring with them:

memories

traditions

reminders

anniversaries

empty chairs

changed dynamics

missing voices

the ache of what used to be

And grief isn't just about losing a person.

There are many forms of grief:

the grief of losing a relationship

the grief of losing the version of yourself you used to know

the grief of dreams that didn't happen

the grief of a friendship that drifted

the grief of time you can't get back

the grief of seasons that changed too quickly

Grief is love with nowhere to go.

And during the holidays, love has everywhere to go — except where you wish it could.

You may find yourself:

crying without warning

withdrawing socially

feeling guilty for having moments of joy

feeling guilty for not having joy

feeling overwhelmed by simple tasks

feeling like everything takes extra emotional energy

missing someone so intensely it feels physical

This is normal.

This is human.

This is grief doing what grief does — moving in waves.

Some waves hit softly.

Some knock the wind out of you.

But hear me:

Grief is not your enemy.

It's the proof that your heart loved deeply.

And yes — you can honor your grief without being swallowed by it.

You can hold sorrow in one hand and hope in the other.

Both can be true.

Both can live in the same heart.

Both can be part of your healing.

"Grief doesn't ruin the holidays.
It simply reminds you that your
heart remembers what mattered."

What No One Tells You About Emotional Triggers

Triggers during the holidays catch you off guard — and they often don't make sense at first.

You might be:

loading groceries into the car

hearing a song in a store

smelling a familiar spice

unpacking decorations

walking past a restaurant

watching a commercial

seeing a couple laugh in public

hearing a phrase your loved one used to say

noticing an empty chair in the corner

...and suddenly your chest tightens.

Your throat warms.

Your eyes sting.

You whisper, "Where did that come from?"

Here's the truth:

Your body remembers before your mind does.

Triggers are not signs you're going backward.

They are signs your heart is trying to process something it didn't have room to process before.

During the holidays:

memories feel closer

senses feel sharper

emotions sit nearer to the surface

And when you are already carrying heaviness, your emotional capacity is lower — meaning what normally feels manageable now feels overwhelming.

Your reaction is not drama.

It's data.

It's your nervous system saying, "Something tender is here."

Your job is not to suppress the trigger.

It's to witness it.

And breathe through it.

And know it will pass.

This is part of the healing.

> *"Triggers don't mean you're broken. They mean your heart still remembers—and is still healing."*

Reflection: A Moment to Pause

• What has felt hardest about this holiday season for me?

• What memories keep rising to the surface?

• Where in my body do I feel heaviness or tightness?

•What am I grieving — even if it's not the kind of loss people talk about?

•What do I wish I could tell someone about what I'm feeling right now?

There are no wrong answers here.

Just truth.

Just you meeting yourself gently.

A Gentle Grounding Exercise (3 Minutes)

Grounding Practice: "Right Here, Right Now"

Sit comfortably. Place one hand over your heart.

Inhale slowly for 4 seconds.

Hold for 2 seconds.

Exhale for 6 seconds.

Whisper to yourself:

"I am safe. I am present. I am allowed to feel this."

Repeat for 3 rounds.

This interrupts emotional spirals and brings your nervous system back into balance.

Closing This Section

You made it through the first emotional layer — acknowledging the heaviness instead of hiding from it.

That's courage.

That's resilience.

That's healing already beginning.

In Chapter 2, we'll gently name the specific weights you've been carrying — not to overwhelm you, but to help you see your inner landscape with clarity and compassion.

Because once you can name your pain, you can begin to navigate it.

And you won't be navigating it alone.

> *"Healing doesn't start when the
> pain ends. Healing starts when
> you stop running from what
> hurts."*

Chapter 2:

Naming the Weight You've Been Carrying

Before you can move through what you're feeling, you have to know what you're actually carrying.

Not the surface emotions.

Not the "I'm fine."

Not the socially acceptable phrases we use to avoid revealing too much.

I'm talking about the deeper layers — the truths you whisper only to yourself.

The unmet expectations.

The quiet disappointments.

The griefs that are not always tied to death, but still cut deep.

The loneliness that's woven into your days like thread you can't quite untangle.

Naming your pain doesn't make it bigger.

It makes it clearer.

And clarity is the first step toward healing.

Because you can't heal what you won't acknowledge.

You can't soothe what you won't name.

You can't release what you refuse to look at.

In this chapter, we'll take a gentle, honest look at what your heart has been managing — maybe for months, maybe for years.

Not to sink into sadness, but to understand what's actually happening inside you.

This is where your power begins to return.

The Many Shapes of Loneliness

Loneliness isn't always isolation.

Sometimes it's the ache of being surrounded by people who don't feel like home.

Sometimes it's waking up in a house that used to be full and now feels too quiet.

Sometimes it's realizing you've outgrown relationships that once meant everything.

Sometimes it's feeling misunderstood in a room full of people who love you dearly.

Loneliness wears different faces:

✔ Emotional Loneliness

You have people — but not people who truly "get you."

✔ Social Loneliness

Your circle has shrunk.

People moved.

Life shifted.

Connections faded.

✔ Situational Loneliness

A specific loss or change left a gap.

A breakup.

A death.

A job transition.

A move.

A child leaving home.

✔ Identity Loneliness

You don't even recognize the person you used to be...

and you're not sure who you're becoming.

Every form of loneliness deserves compassion — especially from you.

*"Loneliness isn't the absence of
people. It's the absence of feeling
seen."*

The Different Faces of Grief

Grief is often misunderstood.

People think it's just sadness.

But grief is layered, complex, unpredictable.

It reaches into the deepest parts of you.

And it isn't limited to losing a loved one — though that grief is profound.

There are many griefs that live in the unseen spaces of your life.

1. Grief of People

Loved ones.

Friends.

Relationships.

Mentors.

People who played chapters of your life but aren't here anymore.

2. Grief of Change

When your life shifts so drastically that it feels like you lost a version of yourself.

3. Grief of Dreams

Things you prayed for.

Hoped for.

Worked for.

Believed for.

And somehow... they didn't happen.

4. Grief of Expectations

The family you imagined.

The marriage you planned.

The career you thought you'd have by now.

The holiday you hoped would feel different.

5. Grief of Innocence or Security

When something painful happened that changed the way you trust, love, or hope.

Each of these is real grief — even if no one else sees it.

And during the holidays, all of them can rise to the surface at once.

Which is why you feel overwhelmed.

Not because you're weak — but because your heart is trying to carry too much alone.

"Some of the deepest griefs have
no obituary. But they deserve to
be honored too."

Why Naming Your Pain Matters

When you name what you're feeling, you're not giving it power — you're taking your power back.

Naming pain:

- calms your nervous system

- reduces emotional confusion

- helps you understand triggers

- brings compassion to the parts of you that feel overwhelmed

- allows you to process instead of suppress

- creates a path forward

Your body already knows you're hurting.

Your heart already knows something feels off.

Naming it simply aligns your mind with the truth your soul has been carrying.

This is where healing begins — not in pretending, but in presence.

Reflection Exercise: "What Am I Really Carrying?"

Take a deep breath. Answer gently.

- What emotions feel closest to the surface right now?

- If I could be honest without fear, what would I say is hurting me the most?

- Which grief feels the heaviest? (Loss of a person, a dream, a season, a relationship?)

- What expectations didn't match reality this year?

- What am I afraid to admit out loud?

- What part of my life feels "not the same," and how is that affecting me?

There is no judgment in these questions.

Just compassion and truth.

The Emotional Inventory: "This Is Where I Am"

Check whichever apply:

☐ I miss someone deeply.

☐ I feel forgotten or overlooked.

☐ I feel disconnected from people I love.

☐ I'm grieving something I can't explain to others.

☐ I feel pressure to "perform" happiness.

☐ I'm exhausted emotionally.

☐ I feel empty even when surrounded by people.

☐ I feel like I'm disappointing someone.

☐ I'm overwhelmed by memories.

☐ I'm afraid to hope again.

☐ I feel stuck in a season I didn't choose.

☐ I don't feel like myself lately.

This inventory is powerful because it will help you identify what's really happening inside — often for the first time.

A Light Faith Reminder: God Sees What Others Don't

You don't have to be deeply religious to feel this truth:

- There is a presence that sees you, even when no one else does.

- A comfort that reaches into the quiet corners of your heart.

- A peace that doesn't erase pain, but sits with you in it.

The Psalms describe God as:

- close to the brokenhearted

- near to those who feel crushed

- a refuge for those who feel overwhelmed

You don't have to understand everything to feel held by something bigger than you.

Let this truth sit with you:

You are not unseen. Not by God. Not by hope. Not by this moment.

Closing This Chapter

You've just taken one of the bravest steps in healing:

you faced your pain instead of outrunning it.

In Chapter 3, we're going to deepen the understanding of your emotional landscape — not to reopen wounds, but to help you gently understand why you feel what you feel so you can begin supporting yourself with compassion instead of judgment.

Because once you can understand your emotional patterns, you can begin shifting them — step by gentle step.

"Clarity isn't the end of pain, but
it is the beginning of peace."

Chapter 3:

You Are Not Broken: Understanding Your Emotional Landscape

There's a moment in every healing journey when you suddenly realize:

"I'm not crazy. I'm not weak. I'm not failing. I'm responding."

Responding to loss.

Responding to disconnect.

Responding to emotional overwhelm.

Responding to memories that didn't wait their turn.

Responding to a season that demands more than your heart has the capacity to give.

This chapter is that moment for you.

You're not broken.

You're not beyond repair.

Your emotions aren't evidence of a flaw — they're evidence of your humanity.

Let's break down what's actually going on inside you... in a way that brings relief, not pressure.

Your Brain Isn't Betraying You — It's Protecting You

When grief or loneliness show up, your brain interprets it as a threat —
even when the "danger" is emotional, not physical.

So it activates:

- hyper-awareness

- fatigue

- emotional sensitivity

- withdrawal

- irritability

- unexpected crying

- a desire to isolate

- trouble concentrating

- difficulty sleeping

- emotional aches that feel physical

This is not failure.

This is your brain's emergency mode trying to shield you.

You're not "too emotional."

Your nervous system is responding to something real.

*"Your emotional reactions aren't
weakness. They're your brain's*

way of saying, 'i'm trying to pro-
tect you.'"

How Your Heart Processes Pain

Your heart processes emotions differently than your mind:

✔ Your mind analyzes pain.

It tries to make sense of what happened, when it happened, why it hurts, and what it means.

✔ Your heart feels pain.

Emotionally.

Deeply.

Non-logically.

Without timelines.

This is why you can understand something logically but still hurt emotionally.

It's not contradiction — it's dual processing.

And during the holidays, your heart works overtime because:

- memories surface

- expectations rise

- comparisons appear

- triggers increase

- emotional bandwidth decreases

So your heart goes into a kind of "gentle overload."

You're not imagining the heaviness.

You're feeling the weight that's been quietly accumulating.

Why Everything Feels More Intense Right Now

Let me explain the science in human language:

During emotionally charged seasons, your adrenaline and cortisol levels fluctuate.

Your serotonin dips.

Your emotional threshold lowers.

Meaning:

What normally rolls off your back now feels heavy.

What normally makes you smile now brings tears.

What normally feels manageable now feels overwhelming.

And that's okay.

You are not meant to "power through" seasons that require tenderness.

The Real Reason Holidays Trigger You

Let's uncover this clearly:

Holidays trigger your emotional past.

Not because you haven't healed...

but because memories and emotions are deeply sensory.

When you:

hear a familiar song

smell something from childhood

see decorations

watch others celebrate

remember someone who's missing

notice a change in family dynamics

experience a quiet moment

...it pulls you into the emotional archives of your heart.

This isn't regression.

It's recall.

It's your heart remembering love.

And loss.

And moments that mattered.

And moments you wish had gone differently.

Your triggers aren't punishing you.

They're revealing the places your heart still cares.

> *"Triggers aren't proof you're stuck. They're proof your heart still remembers."*

Understanding Emotional Waves

Your emotions don't arrive in neat, organized sequences.

They come in waves.

Wave 1: The Sharp Wave

The sudden sadness.

The quick punch of memory.

The unexpected tear.

Wave 2: The Heavy Wave

The fatigue.

The emptiness.

The "I don't want to do anything" feeling.

Wave 3: The Quiet Wave

You're not crying...

but you're not okay either.

You're just numb, moving through the day.

Wave 4: The Rebuilding Wave

Moments of:

- clarity
- strength

- resilience

- "I think I'm going to be okay"

- soft hope returning

You may cycle through these waves many times.

It doesn't mean you're regressing.

It means you're healing.

Healing is not linear — it's layered.

A Gentle "Normalize This For Me" List

You're not alone if you feel:

- overwhelmed by simple tasks

- like you want to isolate

- sensitive to noise or crowds

- easily triggered

- tired for no reason

- frustrated that you're "not yourself"

- guilty for not feeling festive

- unsure how to express what hurts

- irritated by small things

- confused by sudden emotions

- like you're holding back tears

- like you're just going through the motions

All of this is normal.

All of this is human.

Nothing about you is failing.

A Soft Spiritual Reminder

God doesn't expect you to pretend.

He's not asking you to skip the sadness and jump straight to joy.

Scripture is full of people who:

- cried

- grieved

- questioned

- wrestled

- felt alone

- felt overwhelmed

- asked "Why?"

And every time, God met them where they were — not where people thought they "should" be.

You don't have to pray perfectly.

You don't have to feel hopeful every moment.

You don't have to have deep faith right now.

Just know this:

He is near. Even here. Even now. Even in this.

Reflection Exercise: "Understanding My Emotional Patterns"

- When do my emotions feel strongest? Morning, afternoon, evening?

- What tends to trigger the heaviness most?

- What physical sensations come with my emotions?

- What thoughts or fears repeat themselves?

- What emotions am I avoiding because they feel too big?

- What emotions am I judging myself for feeling?

A Short Grounding Practice — "The Kindness Scan"

Place your hand over your heart.

Ask: *"What part of me needs kindness right now?"*

Sit in silence for 10 seconds.

Whisper: *"It's okay. I'm here."*

Breathe slowly.

Let your shoulders drop.

This practice rewires the "self-protection → self-criticism" cycle into "self-protection → self-compassion."

It's subtle but powerful.

Closing This Chapter

You're beginning to understand the emotional map of your own heart — what triggers you, what drains you, what your brain does under pressure, how grief resurfaces, and why loneliness feels so sharp right now.

This is not information.

This is empowerment.

Because once you understand your emotional patterns, you can begin to support yourself with gentleness instead of judgment.

In Chapter 4, we shift from understanding to action — simple, doable practices that bring comfort, grounding, and small but meaningful relief.

You're not rushing.

You're not forcing.

You're just taking one compassionate step at a time.

> *"You're not broken. You're responding to something your heart remembers."*

Chapter 4:

Everyday Practices That Lift the Heaviness (Even If You Don't Feel Like It Yet)

When you're hurting, people love to give advice that feels impossible.

"Just think positive."

"You gotta keep busy."

"Have faith!"

"Choose joy."

But when your heart is heavy, joy doesn't feel like a choice — it feels like a mountain.

This chapter will not ask you to climb mountains.

It will show you how to take steps.

Real steps.

Small steps.

Human steps.

Because healing happens in increments.

In whispers.

In choices no one else sees.

In practices that gently lift the fog one breath at a time.

These practices are divided into three levels — all equally valid.

You're not "falling behind" if all you can manage is Level 1.

Healing isn't about pace.

It's about presence.

Let's start where you are.

LEVEL 1: Easy Practices (Low Effort, Big Comfort)

These are for the days when energy is low, your emotions feel unpredictable, and you just need something that gets you through today without collapsing under the weight of it.

1. The "Get Through Today" Plan

Pick ONE thing from each category:

One thing that comforts your body

(warm drink, soft blanket, slow breathing, warm shower)

One thing that settles your mind

(quiet music, no social media for an hour, light reading)

One thing that anchors your heart

(a prayer, a verse, a grounding affirmation)

When you're hurting, the goal isn't thriving — it's stabilizing.

2. The Comfort Hour

Give yourself one quiet hour a day (even 20–30 minutes works) where you do something kind for yourself.

This could be:

- sitting by a window
- lighting a candle
- watching something gentle
- journaling emotions you didn't say out loud
- listening to calming instrumental music
- listening to worship music
- reading a favorite scripture or verse
- taking a slow walk

You're sending a message to your inner world:

"I'm not abandoning you. I'm here."

3. Sensory Grounding

When heaviness turns into overwhelm, anchor yourself in your senses.

- **5** things you can see
- **4** you can touch
- **3** you can hear
- **2** you can smell

- **1** you can taste

This interrupts emotional spirals by bringing your brain back into your body.

4. Allow Yourself to Pause

Grief and loneliness are exhausting.

Sometimes the most healing thing you can do is nothing.

Rest is not avoidance.

Rest is repair.

5. Put On "Match Then Lift" Music

Start with music that matches your mood.

Then, slowly shift into something slightly lighter — not upbeat, just softer.

This guides your emotions instead of trying to force them.

> *"You don't have to feel better to be-*
> *gin healing. You just have to choose*
> *one gentle thing."*

LEVEL 2: Intermediate Practices (A Little Stretch, Gentle Activation)

These practices create movement — emotional, physical, spiritual — without overwhelming you.

1. Micro-Habits

Tiny, consistent habits help you feel more grounded.

Examples:

- morning affirmation
- lighting a candle during prayer
- writing one sentence in a journal
- 3 deep breaths before bed
- gratitude for one tiny thing

These habits teach your nervous system:

"There is stability here."

2. Connection Touchpoints

Loneliness thrives in silence.

You don't need deep conversation — just consistent touchpoints.

Try:

- sending a text to one safe person
- replying to a message you ignored
- scheduling a short call
- stepping outside where other humans exist
- saying hello to someone at the store

Small signals of connection remind your heart that you're not floating alone.

3. Create Small Pockets of Joy

This is not toxic positivity — it's emotional hope-building.

Choose something tiny:

- your favorite treat

- a cozy show

- a warm beverage

- a soothing scent

- a short walk

- a song that feels like a hug

Let joy be a visitor, not a performance.

4. Decluttering Emotional Noise

Sometimes grief gets louder because life is cluttered — physically and mentally.

Pick one of these:

- clean one drawer

- fold one basket

- delete 10 emails

- organize your nightstand

- wash your favorite mug

The goal isn't productivity.

It's creating a little breathing room.

5. Choose One Moment of Beauty

Beauty softens emotional edges.

Every day, pause and notice one beautiful thing:

- the sky

- a leaf

- a piece of art

- a kind stranger

- sunlight on your wall

Beauty reminds your soul that even in pain, life still holds softness.

> *"Joy doesn't erase sorrow. But it*
> *gives sorrow somewhere soft to*
> *land."*

LEVEL 3: Deeper Work (Heart Work)

These practices are more reflective — do them only when you feel emotionally steady enough.

These aren't quick fixes. They're growth.

1. Release Guilt Around Moving Forward

Grief tries to convince you that:

- laughing means betrayal

- smiling means forgetting

- hope means disloyalty

None of this is true.

You can honor what you lost while still allowing yourself to live.

Give yourself permission to feel moments of light without apologizing for them.

2. Allow Joy Back In — Slowly

Joy is not disrespect to grief.

Joy is proof that healing is happening.

Let joy return at its own pace.

Not forced.

Not faked.

Just allowed.

3. Process the Waves

Don't fear your waves — learn your waves.

Ask:

- What triggered this?

- What do I need right now?

- What part of me is hurting?

- What is this emotion trying to teach me?

Naming the wave reduces its intensity.

4. Uncover the Stories You Tell Yourself

Pain often creates internal narratives:

"I'm too much."

"I'm alone."

"Nothing will get better."

"Everyone else is ahead of me."

"I should be stronger."

Challenge these stories—not with "toxic positivity," but with truth.

Ask yourself:

"What is actually true?"

5. Practice Emotional Permission

Give yourself permission to:

- cry

- rest

- feel

- grieve

- hope

- heal

Permission is liberation.

> *"Your heart is not meant to stay*
> *wounded forever. It's meant to*
> *heal — slowly, steadily, and with*
> *honor."*

Reflection Exercise: "Which Level Am I At Today?"

☐ I need Level 1 — gentle comfort.

☐ I need Level 2 — soft activation.

☐ I need Level 3 — deeper reflection.

Let the answer change daily.

Healing isn't linear; it's responsive.

Spiritual Note for This Chapter

God isn't asking you to leap.

He's inviting you to step.

To breathe.

To rest.

To notice the grace in small beginnings.

He knows your pace — and He honors it.

Closing This Chapter

You've just learned something life-changing:

Healing doesn't require heroic effort.

It requires gentle consistency.

Whether you choose a Level 1 comfort, a Level 2 activation, or a Level 3 reflection...

every small choice is movement.

Every movement is progress.

Every bit of progress is healing.

In Chapter 5, we shift into honoring the person or season you've lost — in ways that bring comfort, not collapse.

Chapter 5:

When You Miss Someone: Honoring Loved Ones Without Losing Yourself

There are some absences that feel louder during the holidays.

You think you're doing okay... until a song plays, or a smell drifts through the room, or you see a family gathered around a table, and suddenly your chest tightens with a familiar ache.

Missing someone during the holidays is its own kind of grief — tender, complex, unpredictable, sacred.

You're not just missing their presence.

You're missing:

- their laugh
- their voice
- their advice
- their favorite foods
- the way they decorated
- the way they prayed
- the way they entered a room

- the way they made you feel like home

- the version of yourself you were with them

Grief isn't a sign you failed to move on.

Grief is the evidence that something mattered — deeply.

And the holidays pull that truth to the surface.

This chapter is about honoring that love... without letting grief swallow you whole.

Your Love Didn't End — It Changed Forms

A lot of people think grief is the end of love.

But actually, grief is what love becomes when the person you love is no longer physically here.

The love didn't disappear.

It shifted.

It deepened.

It settled into the cracks of your heart in a way that both hurts and heals.

Grief isn't the enemy.

It's the echo of love trying to find a place to live.

You don't stop missing someone because time passes.

You start learning how to carry the missing differently.

Some days it feels heavy.

Some days it feels soft.

Some days it sneaks up and surprises you.

Some days it feels achingly beautiful.

You're not doing grief wrong — you're doing it humanly.

"Grief is love with no place to go —
until you give it a place to rest."

Why Holidays Intensify Missing Someone

Holidays are emotional amplifiers.

They amplify:

- memories

- traditions

- family dynamics

- expectations

- absence

- silence

- longing

And when someone you love is missing, holidays become both a celebration and a reminder.

You might feel:

- guilty for feeling joy

- guilty for not feeling joy

- overwhelmed by memories

- detached from celebrations

- afraid of "forgetting"

- afraid of "moving on"

- protective of your grief

- unsure how to interact with family

- angry at the unfairness

- deeply nostalgic

All of these are normal.

All of these are allowed.

You're not supposed to feel one single thing.

You're supposed to feel what's real.

How to Honor Your Loved One Without Collapsing Into Grief

You don't have to choose between:

remembering them

and

taking care of yourself.

You can do both.

Below are gentle ways to honor the person you miss — not to reopen wounds, but to give your love a place to land.

Choose whichever feel right.

Skip whatever doesn't.

This is your journey.

1. Keep a Tradition — Even a Small One

You don't have to recreate everything.

Choose one tradition they loved.

Maybe it's:

- a favorite dish

- a song

- a prayer

- a candle

- a movie

- a decoration

- a phrase they used to say

This isn't about perfection.

It's about connection.

2. Create a New Ritual

New rituals don't replace old memories — they honor them.

Consider:

- lighting a candle in their memory

- writing them a letter

- setting out a photo

- saying a prayer of gratitude

- visiting a place they loved

- sharing a favorite memory

New rituals create a bridge between what was and what is.

3. Tell Their Story

Say their name.

Share their quirks.

Talk about what made them laugh.

Pass down recipes.

Tell the stories that make your heart glow.

When you share memories, you keep them alive in a different way.

And your heart needs that.

4. Give Yourself Permission to Feel the Waves

Missing someone does not make you weak.

It makes you human.

It makes you connected.

It makes you someone who loved deeply.

You're allowed to:

- tear up

- pull away for a moment

- laugh unexpectedly

- feel joy even in your grief

- feel grief even in your joy

Both are allowed.

Both belong.

5. Lean Into Connection When You Can

Grief isolates.

Connection grounds.

You don't need to pour your heart out.

Just let someone be near.

A soft conversation.

A gentle hug.

A shared moment.

A silent presence.

Sometimes the holiest thing you can do is let someone sit with you in your missing.

6. Release the Pressure to Perform

You don't have to:

- be the strong one

- be the cheerful one

- hide your sadness

- pretend you're okay

- make the holiday perfect for others

Your heart is allowed to be where it is.

Without explanation.

Without apology.

> *"Honoring someone you lost is not weakness — it's love remembering."*

For Those Grieving Silent Losses

Not all grief is tied to death.

Some griefs are invisible:

- the relationship that ended

- the marriage that shifted

- the friendship that slowly faded

- the parent you never truly had

- the child you hoped for

- the season that closed

- the identity you had to let go

- the dream that didn't happen

These losses deserve just as much compassion.

You're allowed to grieve the things that didn't turn out the way you imagined.

You're allowed to miss what could have been.

This grief is real.

This grief is valid.

This grief is allowed a seat at the table too.

Reflection Exercise: "How Can I Honor Who or What I Lost?"

- What do I miss most about this person or season?

- What tradition or ritual helps me feel connected to them?

- What new practice could honor their memory?

- What story or moment still brings me comfort?

- What am I afraid to feel — and why?

- Where can I allow myself more compassion this holiday?

A Light Faith Reflection

God doesn't rush your grief.

He doesn't silence it.

He doesn't shame it.

Scripture says He collects tears — meaning your sadness is noticed, valued, held.

The presence of grief doesn't mean the absence of God.

If anything, it means the presence of love.

Let this truth settle in:

You are held in places where you feel most emptied.

Closing This Chapter

Missing someone doesn't mean you're stuck in the past.

It means your love was real.

It means your heart knows how to hold deep connection.

It means you are capable of love that lasts beyond circumstances.

And now, you are learning how to carry that love with honor — without being buried underneath it.

In Chapter 6, we shift into a different lens:

supporting the people who love someone who's hurting — and how to help others show up for you in ways that truly matter.

Chapter 6:

For the Ones Who Love Someone Who Is Hurting

When someone you love is grieving, hurting, or feeling lonely during the holidays, it can be hard to know what to say.

You don't want to make it worse.

You don't want to overstep.

You don't want to disappear either.

You want to show up — but you're scared of showing up wrong.

And if you're the one hurting, you may feel caught between wanting support and not wanting to be a burden.

This chapter bridges that gap.

This chapter teaches people how to show up for someone who's hurting...

and teaches the reader how to receive support without apology.

Because healing isn't meant to happen in isolation.

We're wired for community — even when pain tries to convince us otherwise.

Let's start with the honest truth:

Most people are not uncaring.

They're just unequipped.

This chapter changes that.

What Hurting People Often Wish Understood

When someone is grieving, lonely, or emotionally overwhelmed, their needs shift — even if they don't always say it out loud.

Here's what hurting people usually wish others understood:

✔ "I'm not always in the mood to talk, but I still want to know I matter."

Silence doesn't always mean "leave me alone."

Sometimes it means "stay near — gently."

✔ "I don't want to be fixed. I want to be understood."

Your presence is more healing than your solutions.

✔ "Please don't avoid me because you don't know what to say."

Avoidance deepens the ache — even when it's unintentional.

✔ "My emotions might feel unpredictable, even to me."

That doesn't make them dramatic.

It makes them human.

✔ "Small gestures mean more than you realize."

A text.

A hug.

A thoughtful message.

A warm meal.

A check-in.

These things go a long way.

Hurting people aren't asking for miracles.

Just gentleness.

Just presence.

Just care.

> *"When someone is hurting, your presence matters more than your perfection."*

What to Say (Supportive Phrases That Actually Help)

People fear saying the wrong thing, but support doesn't require perfect wording — just honesty and care.

Here's what truly helps:

✔ *"I'm thinking of you today. No need to respond."*

This removes pressure while still offering connection.

✔ *"You don't have to pretend with me."*

Gives permission to be real.

✔ *"If you want company, I'm here. If you want space, I'm here too."*

Respects emotions without assumptions.

✔ *"I don't have the perfect words, but I'm not going anywhere."*

Reassures them you won't vanish.

✔ *"How can I support you today?"*

Invites clarity and choice.

✔ *"I love you. I'm here."*

Simple. Solid. Human.

These are the phrases people remember.

These are the phrases people hold onto.

What Not to Say (Avoid These Without Judgment)

These are often said with good intentions — but they can unintentionally deepen pain.

Avoid:

"At least they're in a better place."

"Everything happens for a reason."

"You'll get over it."

"Be strong."

"You should be grateful."

"Time heals everything."

"Other people have it worse."

"Don't cry."

"You're still young — you'll find someone."

"You should move on by now."

Why avoid them?

Because they minimize pain instead of making room for it.

People don't need perspective.

They need presence.

> *"Comfort doesn't come from perfect words — it comes from compassionate ones."*

Simple Gestures That Make a Big Difference

Big support is built from small actions.

As a supporter (and reader) choose 1–2 of these:

- drop off a meal

- send a card or handwritten note

- offer a ride or help with errands

- sit with them in silence

- watch a holiday movie together

- help them decorate or undecorate

- bring a warm drink and talk—or don't talk

- send a playlist

- share a memory of their loved one

- check in consistently, not just once

- invite them to something, even if they decline

- send a "thinking of you today" text during important dates

Small touches of kindness become lifelines.

If YOU Are the One Hurting: How to Let People Show Up for You

This is where the empowerment comes in.

Because receiving love can be just as vulnerable as giving it.

✔ 1. You don't have to prove you're okay.

Let people in — just a little.

✔ 2. You're not a burden.

Grief is heavy.

Let someone carry a piece.

Scripture says to bear one another's burdens.

✔ 3. You can ask for something small.

Try:

"Could you check on me this week?"

"Can we talk for 10 minutes?"

"Can you sit with me today?"

Asking isn't weakness — it's wisdom.

✔ 4. You can decline without guilt.

Your emotional bandwidth is limited.

You're allowed to protect it.

✔ 5. You can set boundaries without pushing people away.

Try:

"I love you, and today I need quiet."

"I appreciate the invite — maybe next time."

"I'm just not up for crowds right now."

Boundaries = care, not rejection.

For the Supporters: How to Truly Show Up

This section is a gift to friends and family who WANT to help but don't know how.

✔ Be consistent

Check in regularly.

Not just once.

✔ Be patient

Their healing will not match your timeline.

✔ Be present

You don't have to entertain them.

Just sit with them.

✔ Be flexible

Plans may change based on emotions.

Don't take it personally.

✔ Be a safe space

No pressure.

No platitudes.

No forcing joy.

Just love.

Just care.

Just presence.

> *"The greatest gift you can give someone who is hurting is the space to be themselves without judgment."*

A Light Faith Touch: Showing God's Love Through Presence

Sometimes the most godly thing you can do is simply show up.

Scripture describes love as:

- patient

- kind

- gentle

- present

- honest

- comforting

You don't need perfect prayers to reflect God's heart.

You just need compassion.

Being near someone in their pain is a ministry all by itself.

Reflection Exercise: "Who Can Support Me? Who Can I Support?"

- Who are the safe people in my life right now?

- What kind of support do I need most?

- Who can I gently ask for help?

- Who in my life might also be hurting right now?

- How can I show up for them without overwhelming myself?

Closing This Chapter

You deserve support.

You deserve tenderness.

You deserve people who show up for you gently, consistently, compassionately.

And you deserve to learn how to receive that love without shrinking or apologizing for your needs.

In Chapter 7, we shift into something deeply practical and deeply comforting:

what to do on the days when it all feels like too much.

Those emotional emergencies.

Those nights when the heaviness rolls in fast.

Those mornings when you don't know how to start the day.

We'll build your "emotional emergency kit" — the tools that keep you steady when the waves come.

Chapter 7:

On the Days When It Feels Like Too Much

S ome days the heaviness doesn't knock.

It barges in.

You wake up already tired.

You feel a pressure in your chest or a lump in your throat.

Your thoughts are louder, your emotions are quicker, your patience is thinner.

Maybe you can't stop crying.

Maybe you can't cry at all.

Maybe you feel disconnected from yourself — like you're watching your life instead of living it.

These days don't mean you're failing.

They mean your heart, mind, and body have reached their limit.

And you know what?

It's okay to have limits.

It's okay to have days when everything feels like too much.

This chapter is your soft place to land.

A guide for the moments when you want to hide under the covers, cancel the day, or disappear from the world for a while.

These tools don't "fix" everything — they steady you enough to breathe again.

Let's build your "Break Glass in Case of Emotional Emergency" plan.

Your Emotional Emergency Kit

This isn't a cute self-care list.

This is real, practical, grounding support for emotional overload.

Pick one.

Pick three.

Pick whatever your heart can handle.

1. Sit. Breathe. Put Your Hand Over Your Heart.

When the world feels like too much, your heart needs your presence more than your productivity.

Try this:

- place your hand over your chest

- breathe in for 4

- pause for 2

- exhale for 6

- whisper: *"I am safe. I am here."*

This signals your nervous system to stand down.

2. Let One Tear Fall (or Let the Ones You Have Flow)

You don't have to cry a lot — even one tear is release.

Holding everything in doesn't make you strong.

Letting it out doesn't make you weak.

Sometimes crying is the body's way of saying,

"I've been carrying too much."

3. The 10-Minute Reset

You don't need an hour.

Just ten minutes.

Choose ONE:

- take a warm shower

- walk outside for fresh air

- sit in silence

- play soft music

- stretch your body

- lay down for 10 minutes with your eyes closed

Ten minutes can change the entire emotional tone of your day.

4. Text Someone Safe: "Today feels heavy."

No long explanation.

No emotional essay.

Just:

"Today feels heavy."

It invites support without pressure.

It keeps you from sinking into isolation.

5. Move Your Body Gently

Not a workout.

Not a fitness moment.

Just movement.

Try:

- walking around your home
- slow stretching
- rocking back and forth
- standing outside for air
- swaying to soft music

Movement tells your body,

"We're not stuck. We're safe."

6. Wrap Yourself in Warmth

Warmth grounds the nervous system.

You're not imagining the comfort.

Try:

- warm blanket

- warm drink

- heated pad

- warm socks

- warm bath

When you're overwhelmed, warmth is medicine.

7. Do One Simple Task

Just one:

- wash your face

- make your bed

- open a window

- drink water

- eat something nourishing

- tidy a small corner

Your brain needs small wins to remind you:

"I can do something."

8. Say the Truth Out Loud

You don't have to be poetic.

Just whisper:

- *"This hurts."*
- *"I'm overwhelmed."*
- *"I miss them."*
- *"I'm tired."*
- *"This is a lot."*

Naming the truth breaks emotional pressure.

9. Tell God Exactly How You Feel

Not fancy.

Not scripted.

Just honest.

"God, I don't feel okay."

"God, I'm overwhelmed."

"God, hold me through this."

God doesn't need polish — He wants presence.

10. Give Yourself Permission to Pause

On heavy days, productivity is not the goal.

Self-preservation is.

You're allowed to:

- rest

- cancel plans

- step away

- say no

- move slowly

- do less

Your worth is not attached to your output.

> *"You don't have to be okay to take
> the next step. You just have to be
> willing."*

The Emotional Spiral Interrupt: "Name, Normalize, Nourish"

One of my frameworks — simple, powerful, and accessible.

1. NAME the emotion.

"What am I feeling right now?"

Sadness? Fear? Anger? Loneliness? Exhaustion?

2. NORMALIZE the reaction.

"It makes sense that I feel this way because..."

Your brain softens when you give context.

3. NOURISH yourself.

"What would feel gentle or supportive right now?"

Tea? Space? Music? Prayer? Food? A friend? Warmth?

It's a 20-second reset.

And yes — it works.

When Your Thoughts Start Spiraling

Overthinking is common when you're overwhelmed.

Here's how to interrupt it:

✔ Ask: *"Is this happening, or am I imagining the worst?"*

This separates reality from fear.

✔ Anchor to the present moment.

What can you:

- see

- touch

- hear

- smell

✔ Write the thought down.

Seeing it on paper reduces its power.

✔ Replace the catastrophic ending with something more neutral.

Not positive.

Just neutral.

Your "In Case of Overwhelm" Phrases

- *"This moment is hard, but it won't last forever."*

- *"I can take the next tiny step."*

- *"It's okay to not feel okay."*

- *"I deserve support."*

- *"I am safe in this moment."*

- *"God is near, even when I don't feel it."*

- *"I'm allowed to rest."*

- *"I can breathe through this."*

These phrases steady your mind and slow emotional waves.

A Short Spiritual Anchor for Hard Days

When you feel overwhelmed, remember:

- God is not disappointed in your sadness.

- He's not impatient with your tears.

- He's not distant from your overwhelm.

Scripture says He is:

- close to the brokenhearted

- near to those who feel crushed

- a refuge in times of trouble

- a shelter in the storm

You don't have to muster faith.

Just whisper the smallest prayer:

"God, be near."

He will.

Reflection Exercise: "How Can I Support Myself Today?"

- What do I need right now: comfort, connection, or calm?

- Which practice in the Emergency Kit feels doable?

- Who can I reach out to with one simple message?

- What emotion is closest to the surface today?

- What can I gently let go of today?

You're not solving your whole life — just supporting yourself today.

Closing This Chapter

Some days will feel heavier than others.

Some waves will rise unexpectedly.

Some mornings will require more grace than plans.

Some nights will require more softness than strength.

These days do not define you.

They do not predict your future.

They do not erase your progress.

They are just days.

And you are learning how to navigate them with tenderness, wisdom, and steadiness.

In Chapter 8, we step into the heart of hope — not the "motivational poster" kind, but the real, lived-in hope that grows quietly in the cracks of grief and loneliness.

Chapter 8:

When Hope Feels Impossible... Start Here

H ope can feel like a foreign language when your heart is heavy.

People say:

- *"Just have hope."*

- *"Keep believing."*

- *"Brighter days are coming."*

- *"God's got you."*

And while those words are well-meaning, sometimes they land like pressure instead of comfort.

When you're grieving, overwhelmed, lonely, or emotionally drained, hope can feel:

- distant

- unrealistic

- exhausting

- confusing

- almost offensive

You might wonder:

- *"How am I supposed to hope for anything when I'm barely holding it together?"*

- *"What if hope disappoints me again?"*

- *"What if nothing changes?"*

- *"What if I don't have the energy to hope?"*

This chapter is not about forcing hope.

It's about redefining it.

Because what most people call hope...

isn't hope at all.

Hope Is Not a Feeling — It's a Direction

Hope isn't about feeling positive.

Hope isn't about pretending everything is okay.

Hope isn't about smiling through pain.

Hope is a direction your heart turns toward — even when your emotions aren't caught up yet.

Hope sounds like:

- *"Maybe tomorrow will be softer than today."*

- *"Maybe I can take one more step."*

- *"Maybe I can make room for a little light."*

- *"Maybe I can keep going."*

Hope does not require enthusiasm.

Hope requires willingness.

Willingness to believe that what you feel right now is not the end of your story.

> *"Hope isn't loud. Sometimes it's*
> *the quiet decision to keep going."*

You Don't Need Big Hope — You Need Small Hope

Big hope feels like too much when your heart is tired.

Small hope is sustainable.

Small hope fits in the palm of your hand.

Small hope whispers instead of shouts.

Small hope looks like:

- getting out of bed today

- making a small plan for tomorrow

- imagining a moment of peace

- taking a shower

- texting someone safe

- breathing through the wave

- journaling one sentence

- allowing yourself to laugh once

- noticing beauty in something ordinary

Small hope builds emotional strength quietly — the way roots grow underground before anyone sees the tree.

You don't need giant hope to heal.

You just need one small hope at a time.

Why Hope Feels Hard When You're Hurting

Hope requires vulnerability — the willingness to believe that something good can still happen.

But when you've been disappointed, hurt, or blindsided by life, your brain becomes cautious.

Your subconscious tries to protect you by saying:

- *"Don't expect anything."*

- *"Don't hope too big."*

- *"Don't get your heart broken again."*

- *"Don't trust joy too much."*

Your mind thinks it's keeping you safe.

But it's actually keeping you stuck.

This doesn't mean you're pessimistic or weak.

It means you're human.

It means your heart is recovering.

It means your trust in life is tender right now.

And tender hope is still hope.

The Science of Slowly Returning to Hope

Here's the beautiful truth:

Your brain can learn hope again — the same way it learns fear, grief, or coping.

Through:

- repetition

- gentle moments of truth

- small emotional wins

- safe connections

- moments of beauty

- compassionate internal dialogue

- grounding practices

Hope is something your brain gets better at over time.

You're not starting from scratch.

You're rebuilding strength in the places that were stretched thin.

A Gentle Faith Reflection: Hope That Rises Quietly

Hope in Scripture isn't portrayed as hype.

It's portrayed as:

- an anchor

- a light in the dark

- a small flame that refuses to go out

- steady trust, not loud certainty

Biblical hope isn't about pretending life isn't hard.

It's about believing:

"Even here, God is near."

Even in grief.

Even in loneliness.

Even in unanswered questions.

Even in slow healing.

God doesn't demand your hope — He nurtures it.

You don't have to leap into hope.

You can ease into it.

Slowly.

Gently.

Honestly.

"Hope doesn't deny the darkness
*— it def*ies it.*"*

Tiny Practices That Rebuild Hope (Even When You Don't Feel Like It)

These practices are designed for low emotional bandwidth.

Choose one a day — or one a week.

1. The One Good Thing Practice

Before bed, write down one thing that was good today, even if it was tiny.

This teaches your brain to look for possibility.

2. The "Maybe" Exercise

When fear says: *"Nothing will change,"*

respond with: *"Maybe something will."*

"Maybe today isn't the whole story."

"Maybe I'm more resilient than I feel."

"Maybe healing is happening slowly."

"Maybe" opens the door to hope.

3. The 2-Minute Visual Reset

Close your eyes.

Imagine a warm light.

Imagine breathing it in.

Imagine it filling your shoulders, chest, stomach, arms.

This is not fantasy — it calms your nervous system and signals safety.

4. The "Borrowed Hope" Method

When your hope runs low, borrow someone else's.

Think:

- of a friend who loves you

- of someone who believes in you

- of something God has brought you through

- of something small that has gone right

- of a moment when you felt peace

Borrowed hope still counts.

5. Celebrate Micro-Wins

You took a shower?

That's progress.

You reached out to someone?

Progress.

You ate something nourishing?

Progress.

You got through the day?

That's courage.

Micro-wins rebuild internal strength.

Reflection Exercise: "Where Is Hope Already Showing Up?"

- What tiny thing gave me comfort today?

- What small moment made me breathe easier?

- What beauty did I notice this week?

- What fear turned out differently than I imagined?

- What is one thing I can look forward to, even if it's small?

- Your mind might not call these "hope" yet — but your heart knows better.

Closing This Chapter

Hope doesn't return as a flood.

It returns as a drip.

A flicker.

A whisper.

A tug at your heart reminding you that something beautiful is still possible.

You don't have to force it.

You don't have to manufacture it.

You just have to stay open to the possibility that:

- Life is not done giving you good things.

- Your heart is not done healing.

- Your story is not done unfolding.

In Chapter 9, we step into rebuilding —

one day at a time, one choice at a time, one moment of courage at a time.

Chapter 9:

One Day at a Time: Building Your Way Out of the Dark

Y ou don't climb out of emotional heaviness in one leap.

You don't heal in one revelation.

You don't rebuild your life in one triumphant moment.

You rebuild slowly.

Steadily.

Quietly.

One small step at a time.

And the truth is simple but life-changing:

You don't need to know the whole path to take the next step.

This chapter is about the next step — not the whole staircase.

Healing Happens in Small, Repeatable Movements

Hollywood sells transformation as a sudden breakthrough.

Real life?

Breakthrough happens drop by drop.

Small shifts.

Small habits.

Small decisions that slowly rewire your heart and mind.

Your healing will come from:

- consistency

- gentleness

- honesty

- patience

- micro-changes

- compassionate routines

These are the foundations that help you navigate out of the dark and into sturdier emotional ground.

Let's walk through them.

Rebuilding Emotional Stamina

Emotional stamina is not about strength.

It's about the ability to stay present with yourself — especially when emotions rise.

You build emotional stamina through small acts of courage, like:

- acknowledging what hurts

- slowing down instead of shutting down

- letting someone support you

- choosing a tiny action when you feel stuck

- noticing the progress you didn't think mattered

Deep healing requires deep presence — not deep pressure.

Identity Rebuilding After Loss

Grief and loneliness don't just affect how you feel — they affect who you believe you are.

Pain shakes your identity.

It questions your worth.

It makes you wonder if you'll ever feel like "you" again.

But here's the truth:

- You are not lost.

- You are evolving.

And grief is shaping the next version of you with strength you can't see yet.

Identity rebuilding begins with three truths:

1. You Are Still You — Just a Softer, Wiser You

The pain didn't erase you.

It refined you.

2. You Don't Have to Go Back to Who You Were

You're allowed to grow forward, not backward.

3. You Get to Redefine Yourself Slowly

Not in one go.

Not under pressure.

But gently, as your heart opens again.

> *"You haven't lost yourself — you're*
> *meeting a new version of you."*

Choosing Life Again — Gently, Intentionally, Slowly

Choosing life doesn't mean feeling happy.

It means choosing:

- connection over isolation

- rest over shutdown

- reflection over avoidance

- small joy over emotional numbness

- movement over stagnation

- truth over self-judgment

These choices accumulate.

They become strength.

They become healing.

Each small step is a vote for your future self — the version of you who's learning to breathe again.

The "One Good Thing" Daily Practice

This simple practice shifts your emotional baseline over time.

Every day, write down one good thing that happened.

Not extraordinary.

Not groundbreaking.

Just good.

Examples:

- someone smiled at you

- the sky was pretty

- your tea tasted comforting

- you felt a moment of peace

- you took a deep breath that felt grounding

- you remembered something sweet

- you laughed

- you rested without guilt

One good thing is not about pretending life is perfect.

It's about noticing the moments of light breaking through the heaviness.

Momentum Comes from Micro-Movements

Stop trying to overhaul your life.

Just do one thing each day that moves you forward.

Ideas for micro-movements:

- drink water with intention

- tidy one small space

- send a text to a friend

- step outside for fresh air

- stretch for 3 minutes

- write one sentence in a journal

- practice one grounding breath

- read a comforting verse

- take a 5-minute walk

Every small movement counts.

Healing is a collection of little yeses.

A Gentle Push Toward Hopeful Action

This is not the "hustle chapter."

This is the "you're ready to step again" chapter.

Ask yourself:

- What is one thing I can do today that honors my healing?

- What is one thing I've been avoiding that would help me

breathe again?

- What is one simple action that moves me 1% forward?

You don't need a plan.

You just need one step.

Your "One Day at a Time" Framework

1. TODAY I WILL NOTICE

One moment of beauty.

One moment of ease.

One moment of comfort.

2. TODAY I WILL CHOOSE

One simple step that supports me.

3. TODAY I WILL REMEMBER

I don't need to be healed to be healing.

4. TODAY I WILL REST

At least once — without guilt.

5. TODAY I WILL BELIEVE

Not in perfection...

but in possibility.

*"You don't need to see the whole
road to take one brave step."*

A Light Faith Touch: God Walks at Your Pace

God isn't rushing you toward joy.

He's walking with you toward it.

Step.

By step.

By step.

Sometimes His presence feels like a whisper.

Sometimes like a warmth.

Sometimes like a pause that makes room for peace.

You don't need to sprint back to life.

You're allowed to heal at the pace of grace.

Reflection Exercise: "What Is My Next Right Step?"

What's one simple thing I can do today that would support my heart?

- What's one thing I can let go of for today?
- What's one small action that feels hopeful?
- What feels possible for me right now — even if it's tiny?
- Who can I reach out to for a moment of connection?

- These tiny reflections build clarity — and clarity builds momentum.

Closing This Chapter

You don't climb your way out of the dark by focusing on the top.

You climb by focusing on the next foothold.

You rebuild your life:

- one breath

- one step

- one small act

- one moment of courage

- one day at a time

You're not behind.

You're not failing.

You're not stuck.

You're becoming.

And the next chapter — Chapter 10 — brings it all together.

It's the crescendo of the book.

The moment where we look forward, gently but boldly, into who you are becoming and the life that is still calling your name.

Chapter 10:

You Are Still Becoming: A New Season Is Calling You Forward

Y ou've walked through heaviness.

You've faced grief with honesty.

You've named your loneliness.

You've steadied yourself in the emotional storms.

You've learned what your heart needs.

You've taken small steps toward hope.

You've rebuilt pieces of your strength.

And here you are — reading this final chapter.

Not because everything is perfect now.

Not because the heaviness has magically disappeared.

Not because life suddenly feels easy.

But because something in you — the quiet, resilient part you sometimes forget about — kept going.

And that matters.

It matters more than you know.

This chapter is not about pretending the pain is gone.

It's about recognizing this truth:

- You are not the same person who opened this book.

- You are becoming someone softer, wiser, braver, steadier, and more open to the life ahead of you.

This chapter is your gentle reminder of that becoming.

You Don't Have to Be "Healed" to Move Forward

Healing isn't a finish line.

It's a direction.

A posture.

A daily decision to keep living, even when some days feel heavier than others.

You don't have to:

- feel whole to take a step

- feel strong to try again

- feel hopeful to move forward

- feel confident to rebuild

- feel joyful to receive joy

- You don't need to reach 100% to begin.

You can move forward at 12%, 37%, 52%, or 77%.

Progress is not measured in emotional percentages.

Progress is measured in willingness.

And you, right here, reading this?

You are willing.

> *"You don't move forward once you're healed — you move forward because healing happens along the way."*

Let Yourself Dream Again (Slowly)

Dreaming feels risky when you've been hurt.

It feels vulnerable.

It feels tender.

But dreaming is not reckless.

Dreaming is a sign of life.

This isn't about big dreams or perfect plans.

This is about soft, quiet dreams — the kind that whisper instead of shout.

Ask yourself:

- What is one thing I hope to experience again?

- What is one thing I want to feel again?

- What is one thing I want to create in this next season?

- What is one thing I want to reclaim?

- What is one thing I want to try — even if it scares me?

Your heart is stretching again — not with urgency, but with possibility.

Build a Future You Want to Walk Into

You don't have to build the whole future at once.

You just build pieces of it.

Steady pieces.

Hopeful pieces.

Honest pieces.

Examples:

- reconnect with someone safe

- take one step toward a personal goal

- add one healthy habit

- remove one draining pattern

- revisit something that once brought joy

- try something new that feels good

- open your life to community again

- revisit your spirituality with fresh curiosity

- make space for rest and pleasure

Your future doesn't need to be perfect.

It just needs to be yours.

You Are Allowed to Feel Joy Again

This one might feel the most vulnerable.

You may feel:

- guilty for laughing

- nervous about feeling good

- afraid joy won't last

- unsure if you're "ready"

But hear this clearly:

- Joy does not dishonor your grief.

- Joy does not erase your love.

- Joy does not betray your past.

- Joy means you're alive.

- Joy means you're healing.

- Joy means your heart is making room for light again.

You deserve moments of joy — even tiny ones.

Even surprising ones.

Even fragile ones.

Let them in slowly.

Let them expand gently.

Let them return in their own time.

*"Joy is not a betrayal of what
you've lost — it's proof that you're
still living."*

Recognizing Your Own Strength

You may not feel strong.

You may not feel brave.

You may not feel resilient.

But look at what you've survived.

Look at what you've faced.

Look at what you've carried.

Look at how you've kept going.

Strength is not loud.

Strength is quiet consistency in the face of heaviness.

Strength is waking up on days when you wanted to stay in bed.

Strength is holding onto faith the size of a mustard seed.

Strength is breathing through waves that once drowned you.

Strength is learning to be gentle with yourself.

You are stronger than you feel.

More resilient than you think.

More capable than you realize.

Your Becoming Is Not Finished

Life after grief, loneliness, or hard seasons isn't about "getting back to normal."

It's about becoming — becoming someone:

- grounded

- present

- open

- wise

- resilient

- compassionate

- steady

- connected

- hopeful

You are not returning to who you once were.

You are growing into who you are designed to be next.

And that version of you?

She's beautiful.

Strong.

Soft.

Depth-filled.

More available to joy.

More anchored in truth.

More connected to herself.

More aware of God's nearness.

More open to love.

More comfortable in her own skin.

She is already emerging.

A Gentle Blessing for Your Next Season

May your steps be steady.

May your days be softer.

May your nights be peaceful.

May your heart find room to rest.

May light find you gently.

May love return slowly.

May joy surprise you again.

May hope rise in small, quiet ways.

May the memory of what you've lost be honored.

May your faith deepen and expand.

May compassion wrap around you.

May you walk into your next season with courage.

And may you never forget:

- You are healing.

- You are becoming.

And you are not alone — not now, not ever.

Reflection Exercise: "Who Am I Becoming?"

- What qualities are emerging in me through this season?

- What have I learned about myself?

- What strengths surprised me?

- What do I want to bring into my next chapter?

- What can I leave behind?

- What does "becoming" look like for me right now?

Your healing isn't about the past you lost — it's about the future you're still growing into.

Closing This Book

Take one deep breath.

You made it through the heaviness.

You made it through the ache.

You made it through the questions.

You made it through the memories.

You made it through the quiet nights and the heavy mornings.

And now...

You're standing in a new kind of space —

a space where you are no longer defined by your pain,

but shaped by your courage.

This isn't the end of your healing.

It's the beginning of your becoming.

Afterword

From My Heart to Yours

If you're reading these final pages, it means you stayed with this journey all the way through — page by page, emotion by emotion, breath by breath.

That tells me something important about you:

You are stronger, softer, braver, and more resilient than you realize.

This book wasn't written to erase your pain or rush your healing.

It was written to hold space for your humanity — the kind of space where grief can breathe, hope can flicker, and your heart can slowly come back to life.

If you take nothing else with you, let it be this:

You were never broken.

You were never behind.

You were never alone.

You have been becoming — even in the dark.

Your tears watered something inside you that is now ready to grow.

Your quiet courage carried you when nothing else could.

And now, you are stepping into a new chapter.

Maybe slowly.

Maybe gently.

But stepping, nonetheless.

Give yourself grace.

Give yourself time.

Give yourself room to keep healing, loving, learning, laughing, and re-discovering the parts of yourself that grief or loneliness tried to dim.

Your story is not over.

Your heart is not done rising.

Your light is not done shining.

Thank you for letting me walk with you.

It has been an honor to hold a bit of your heart on these pages.

May you carry forward not just hope —

but the deep, unshakable truth that you are worthy of joy, peace, healing, and a future filled with good things.

You are still becoming.

And the world is better because you're still here.

— Pat

Acknowledgments

To every person who has carried quiet pain through loud seasons — this book is for you.

Thank you for trusting these pages with parts of your heart you rarely reveal.

To my readers who show up in their humanity, honesty, and vulnerability:

you are the reason I write.

You are the reason this work exists.

Your courage inspires me every single day.

To my **Breakthrough Coaching Experience** community — past, present, and future — thank you for allowing me to walk beside you through seasons of growth, grief, transition, resilience, and breakthrough.

Your stories shape my purpose.

Your strength reminds me why this work matters.

To my **Do. Say. Be. ™ Breakthrough Podcast** listeners — your messages, stories, and testimonies breathe life into this mission.

Thank you for tuning in, showing up, and allowing your own breakthroughs to ripple out into the world.

To my family and loved ones — thank you for being my grounding force.

Your prayers, your love, and your unwavering belief in me are gifts I do not take lightly.

To my clients, students, and every soul I've coached through life's storms:

you taught me the language of resilience, the rhythm of steady hope, and the sacred power of human connection.

So much of what's in this book comes from the lessons you've lived.

And to God — for Your nearness, Your peace, Your steadying presence, even when life felt heavy.

For whispering hope into my spirit when I needed it most and guiding me to write words that would become comfort for others.

Thank you — truly — for letting me be part of your healing journey.

Turning Pages Into Healing

Your Next Steps...

Reading this book was an act of courage.

But the real transformation begins when these words move from the page into your everyday life.

This section gives you a simple, clear, compassionate path forward — something you can hold onto even when the emotions rise again or the world feels overwhelming.

You don't need to memorize everything.

You don't need to do it all at once.

Just take the next gentle step.

Here are a few places to begin.

1. Choose One Practice From the Book to Start With

Go back through the chapters and choose one thing — just one — that you can begin practicing this week.

Maybe it's:

the grounding breath

your "Comfort Hour"

the "One Good Thing" practice

the "Name–Normalize–Nourish" exercise

daily micro-rituals

the 10-minute reset

choosing one moment of beauty

Pick the one that feels doable.

Not the one that feels impressive.

The one that feels sustainable.

Healing grows from consistency, not intensity.

2. Create a "Good Days / Hard Days" Routine

Your emotional landscape will shift — and that's okay.

A simple way to support yourself is to create two routines:

✔ For Good Days

When you're feeling lighter:

- step outside
- connect with a friend
- add one small goal to your day
- try something that brings joy

✔ For Hard Days

When the heaviness comes:

- slow your pace

- breathe deeply

- use your Emergency Kit from Chapter 7

- speak gently to yourself

- rest without guilt

This isn't about performing.

It's about honoring your real capacity.

3. Build a Support Circle (Even a Small One)

You don't need a big community — you just need a safe one.

Choose one to three people you can be honest with.

People who hold space without judgment.

People who check in without pressure.

People who show up with tenderness.

Let them know what you need:

- *"Sometimes I just need a listening ear."*

- *"Sometimes I may need space, and that's okay."*

- *"Sometimes I need a reminder that I'm not alone."*

Support doesn't weaken you — it steadies you.

4. Give Yourself Permission to Rest and Recover

You've been carrying a lot.

Even emotional healing takes energy.

Let yourself:

- nap

- step away

- unplug

- breathe

- reset

- take breaks

- say no

- postpone plans

- move slowly

Rest is not a luxury — it's survival.

It's self-respect.

It's what gives your heart room to heal.

5. Journal Through the Reflection Prompts

The reflection questions scattered throughout this book are doorways into deeper clarity.

Choose one chapter each week and journal through the prompts.

This helps you:

- process emotions

- track growth

- understand patterns

- soften self-judgment

- build self-awareness

- release emotional tension

Your journal becomes your emotional companion — a place for honesty, softness, and truth.

6. Begin Rebuilding Your Life One Day at a Time

Use the "One Day at a Time" framework from Chapter 9:

- Today I will notice...

- Today I will choose...

- Today I will remember...

- Today I will rest...

- Today I will believe...

You don't need to feel inspired to do this.

Just present.

Just willing.

Little steps create real change.

7. Turn Back to This Book When You Need Support

This isn't a "read once and forget it" kind of book.

It's a companion.

A guide.

A soft place to land on nights when the heaviness returns.

A grounding presence on mornings when you feel overwhelmed.

Come back to:

- Chapter 1 when emotions feel sharp

- Chapter 3 when you feel broken

- Chapter 4 when you need comfort

- Chapter 7 on the hard days

- Chapter 9 when you need momentum

- Chapter 10 when you need hope again

Let these chapters hold you, remind you, and steady you whenever you need it.

8. Consider Going Deeper With Guidance and Support

Sometimes healing requires help.

Not because you're weak — but because you're human.

If you're ready for deeper transformation, greater clarity, or personalized support, I'd be honored to walk with you through the next steps of your journey.

You'll find invitations and resources in the pages ahead — for coaching, community, and continued growth.

You don't have to do this alone.

"Transformation doesn't happen in one leap — it happens in one gentle, honest step at a time."

About The Author

Patricia Hylton is a Certified HR Executive, leadership strategist, and transformational coach who has spent over two decades helping people rise — in their careers, their lives, their leadership, and their personal seasons of becoming.

As the Founder of The Breakthrough Coaching Experience, she guides professionals, executives, and everyday individuals through moments of uncertainty, transition, grief, stuckness, and reinvention. Her work blends strategy, soul, emotional clarity, and practical forward movement — helping people steady themselves, rebuild confidence, and take bold, purpose-driven action.

Patricia is also the creator and host of The Do. Say. Be.™ Breakthrough Podcast, where she helps listeners move from confusion to clarity, from hesitation to action, and from stuck to breakthrough. Known for her warmth, honesty, and grounding presence, she brings deep insight into the human experience and a gift for making people feel seen, understood, and safe.

Before stepping fully into coaching and speaking, Patricia spent more than twenty years leading People & Culture functions across multiple industries, guiding C-suite leaders, shaping organizational culture, and developing high-performing teams. Her corporate background, combined with her coaching lens, allows her to translate complex emotional and leadership challenges into clear, actionable guidance.

Her signature belief is simple:

"Your breakthrough is already within you — because you were built for more."

Patricia's work sits at the intersection of resilience, clarity, personal transformation, and emotional restoration. She is passionate about supporting people who feel overwhelmed by life's curveballs — from loneliness to loss to career transitions — and helping them rediscover their identity, strength, and God-given potential.

Whether through coaching, writing, speaking, teaching, or podcasting, Patricia shows up with one mission:

to help people navigate life's hardest seasons with steadiness, compassion, clarity, and hope — and to walk with them as they rise into their next chapter.

She currently lives in the U.S., where she continues to build a coaching and media brand devoted to human breakthrough, emotional resilience, and purpose-driven living.

An Invitation To The DO. SAY. BE.™ Breakthrough Podcast

If this book found you in a tender season...

If the chapters met you where life felt heavy...

If something inside you feels a little steadier, a little clearer, a little more hopeful...

Then you'll feel right at home on *The Do. Say. Be.™ Breakthrough Podcast.*

This is where we go even deeper — into the real, messy, beautiful parts of being human.

It's a space for honest conversations, emotional clarity, spiritual grounding, and practical steps that help you move from stuck to breakthrough in every area of your life.

On the podcast, we talk about:

- navigating hard seasons

- rebuilding confidence

- healing emotional wounds

- finding your voice

- processing grief and change

- releasing self-sabotage

- reconnecting with purpose

- developing resilience from the inside out

And we do it with warmth, humor, candor, and compassion — the same energy you felt in these pages.

Every episode is designed to meet you right where you are... and not leave you there.

If this book spoke to you, the podcast will carry you even further — one conversation at a time, one truth at a time, one breakthrough at a time.

 Listen on **YouTube**, **Apple Podcasts**, **Spotify**, or your favorite streaming platform.

Just search for *The Do. Say. Be.* ™ *Breakthrough Podcast.*

I'll meet you there — with clarity, care, and the same steady presence you felt here.

An Invitation To Go Deeper

The Breakthrough Coaching Experience

If this book touched something tender in you...

If you recognized yourself in these pages...

If you felt seen, understood, or steadied in ways you didn't expect...

You don't have to navigate this next season alone.

For many people, healing begins with awareness — but true transformation happens with support.

That's where *The Breakthrough Coaching Experience* comes in.

This is the heart of my work:

- walking with people through the parts of life that feel heavy, confusing, or overwhelming...

- and helping them find clarity, confidence, resilience, and purpose on the other side.

Whether you are:

- rebuilding after loss

- navigating loneliness

- healing from emotional exhaustion

- reinventing yourself

- stepping out of a stuck season

- craving clarity about what's next

- or simply wanting to feel whole again

...coaching gives you a structured, caring place to do the inner work with guidance, tools, and accountability.

What Coaching With Me Looks Like

You can expect:

- a calm, steady presence

- honest but gentle conversation

- real tools for emotional healing

- deeply personalized strategies

- clarity you can actually use

- forward movement (without overwhelm)

- a space where all parts of you are welcome

This is not quick-fix coaching.

It's soul-level work.

Strategic work.

The kind that helps you rise from the inside out.

Together, we'll work through a blend of:

- emotional clarity

- resilience building

- purpose alignment

- mindset shifts

- identity rebuilding

- gentle accountability

- practical next steps

- spiritual grounding (light, invitational, honoring your pace)

You bring your honesty.

I'll bring my guidance.

We'll build your next chapter together.

If you're ready for more support...

You can learn about 1:1 coaching, group programs, and upcoming offerings at:

www.TheBreakthroughCoachingExperience.com

Or connect with me directly for next steps:

Email: info@TheBreakthroughCoachingExperience.com

Your life may feel heavy now... but your healing, your clarity, and your becoming are already unfolding.

I would be honored to walk this part of the journey with you.

Recommended Resources

For Healing, Hope, and Emotional Restoration

These resources are here for the days when your heart feels heavy, the nights when your thoughts feel loud, and the moments when you need something steady to hold on to.

You don't have to use them all at once — just choose what feels gentle, supportive, and doable in this season.

Books for Emotional Healing & Grief

These are grounded, compassionate, faith-aware, and emotionally safe — perfect for gentle seasons of healing.

It's OK That You're Not OK by Megan Devine
One of the most validating books on grief and emotional pain.

The Next Right Thing by Emily P. Freeman
A beautiful guide for taking one small step at a time.

When the Heart Waits by Sue Monk Kidd
Soft, reflective, and deeply grounding.

Try Softer by Aundi Kolber
Gentle trauma-informed care for your emotional world.

Boundaries by Dr. Henry Cloud & Dr. John Townsend
A foundational read for self-protection as you heal.

Healing After Loss by Martha Whitmore Hickman
Daily reflections for navigating grief with tenderness.

Faith, Spirituality & Gentle Encouragement

Light-faith references, devotional warmth, and simple grounding truths.

One Minute Inspirations for Women by Elizabeth George

The Bible App (YouVersion) – Offers reading plans for grief, emotional overwhelm, and hope.

Every Moment Holy by Douglas Kaine McKelvey
Liturgies for everyday life, including sorrow, waiting, and healing.

Grace for the Moment by Max Lucado
Small, comforting spiritual reminders.

Guided Journals & Reflection Tools

For emotional processing, clarity, and grounded self-awareness.

The Resilience Reset™ Workbook (available via www.TheBreakthroughCoachingExperience.com)
A powerful tool to steady, rebuild, and restore confidence.

The Next Right Thing Guided Journal by Emily P. Freeman
Start Where You Are by Meera Lee Patel
Visual, creative, and gentle.

Therapist-recommended Blank Journals

Any calming, simple journal will work — choose one that feels safe to write in.

Apps for Mental & Emotional Support

For grounding, breathing, and emotional stabilization.

Calm — Breathing, sleep stories, grounding meditations.

Headspace — Short guided sessions for anxiety, loneliness, and overwhelm.

Abide — Faith-based guided meditations for sleep and peace.

Fabulous — Gentle habit-building for daily emotional support.

Insight Timer — Free meditations for grief, healing, and calming your nervous system.

Support Hotlines (U.S.)

For emotional emergencies — no shame, no judgment, just support.

988 Suicide & Crisis Lifeline: Call or text 988 — free, confidential, 24/7 support.

Crisis Text Line: Text HOME to 741741 for immediate support.

NAMI Helpline: 1-800-950-NAMI (6264) — emotional support & mental health resources.

My Breakthrough Resources

My offerings (current and upcoming) that you can turn to next:

The Do. Say. Be.™ Breakthrough Podcast - available on all podcast platforms (https://www.youtube.com/@do-say-be)

Weekly conversations on resilience, healing, and finding clarity. Supportive online Breakthrough Community.

The Breakthrough Coaching Experience (https://thebreakthroughcoachingexperience.com)

1:1 coaching for clarity, confidence, and emotional steadiness.

The Resilience Reset™ — A guided micro-program for navigating emotional storms with strength.

Breakthrough Journals, Guides, and Devotionals

Your Reflections

What resonated most with me?

_____

_____

_____

_____

_____

_____

What emotions surfaced as I read?

_____

_____

_____

_____

_____

_____

What small truths do I want to remember?

_____

_____

_____

_____

_____

_____

What parts of myself feel different now?

_____

_____

_____

_____

_____

My personal reminders:

_____

_____

_____

_____

_____

My intentions for the next season of my life:

_____

_____

_____

_____

_____

_____

Call-To-Action

If these pages held you...

If they helped you breathe...

If they reminded you that you're not alone...

Then I would love to walk with you in your next chapter of healing and becoming.

Explore coaching, upcoming programs, and supportive resources at:

TheBreakthroughCoachingExperience.com

Connect with me for speaking, interviews, or deeper support at:

info@TheBreakthroughCoachingExperience.com

And join me each week on

The Do. Say. Be.™ Breakthrough Podcast for honest conversations, emotional tools, and life-giving clarity.

Your healing is unfolding — and you don't have to walk it alone.

Final Blessing

For Your Next Chapter

Before you close this book, take one slow breath.

Feel your shoulders drop.

Feel your heart settle.

Feel the gentle truth rising inside you:

You are still here.

And you are still becoming.

May the heaviness you've carried begin to lighten.

May the waves that once felt overwhelming soften with time.

May grace meet you in unexpected moments —

in quiet mornings,

in warm hands,

in small joys,

in whispers of hope.

May you find steady ground beneath your feet again.

May you rediscover laughter without guilt.

May you feel connection returning, slowly and safely.

May you honor what was lost and still make room for what can be gained.

May peace find you gently, without pressure or performance.

And may you walk forward knowing this:

- You are not broken.

- You are not behind.

- You are not alone.

- You are growing — even in the dark.

- You are healing — even in the silence.

- You are rising — even when you can't feel it yet.

May this next season be filled with softness, clarity, courage, and the quiet, steady confidence that your story is still unfolding — and it is not done giving you beauty.

You are held.

You are supported.

You are becoming who you were always meant to be.

Go gently.

Go slowly.

Go in grace.

Your next chapter is waiting for you —

and you are ready for it.

www.ingramcontent.com/pod-product-compliance
Lightning Source LLC
Chambersburg PA
CBHW070933130626
46555CB00001B/408